Contents

W9-AHF-250

Derek Jeter is a superstar in Major League Baseball (MLB). He plays shortstop for the New York Yankees. The team is based in the Bronx, in New York City. The Yankees are often called "The Bronx Bombers." Through 2012, the Yankees had won 27 World Series titles. That is more than any other sports team in history.

Derek Jeter is the captain of the Yankees. He was chosen captain because he is a great leader. He inspires his teammates and is always there for them. Jeter knows that being the captain is a great honor. He once said, "Captain of the Yankees is not a title that I throw around lightly. It is a huge responsibility and one that I take very seriously." In fact, only two other teams in Major League Baseball had official captains at the start of the 2013 season. They were Paul Konerko of the Chicago White Sox and David Wright of the New York Mets.

Jeter celebrates the Yankees 2009 World Series championship. On the right is Yankees co-owner Hal Steinbrenner.

As a shortstop, Jeter plays between second and third base on the field. A shortstop must have a strong arm. He often has to throw the ball across the diamond to the first baseman. The shortstop also has to catch ground balls. That is called fielding. Most players are better at either fielding or hitting. But Jeter is terrific at both! Besides being a great fielder, he is usually one of the league leaders in hits and runs scored.

As a boy, Derek was often called "DJ." Nowadays Derek has other nicknames. He is often called "Captain Clutch" because he comes through when the game is on the line. He is also known as "Mr. November." That is because he plays well at the end of the season in the playoffs and World Series. In fact, through the 2012 season Jeter had a World Series batting average of .321!

Jeter has been playing pro baseball for many years. Each year he seems to get better. Ed Bradley, a reporter with the TV show *60 Minutes*, once said, "(Derek) gets better every year; that's what's remarkable about him. Some guys are good and stay good. Some guys are good and get better."

Derek Sanderson Jeter was born on June 26, 1974 in Pequannock, New Jersey. He was the first child born to Charles Jeter and Dorothy Jeter. Charles earned a living as a drug and alcohol counselor. Dorothy worked as an accountant. The family moved to Kalamazoo, Michigan when Derek was four

Chapter 1

Early Years

years old. The following year, Derek's younger sister, Sharlee, was born. Derek and Sharlee have always been very close.

In the summer, Derek and Sharlee often visited their grandparents in New Jersey. The entire family loved baseball. Their favorite team was the New York Yankees. Derek loved going to games at Yankee Stadium. Soon he became a die-hard Yankees fan. Derek's favorite player was outfielder Dave Winfield.

Derek wanted to play just like Winfield. He spent many hours hitting balls in the backyard with his family. When he was old enough, Derek played Little League ball. Charles coached the team, and often asked Derek to play different positions. Derek wanted to play shortstop. But his dad knew it would be good for Derek to learn to play other positions, too.

While still a young boy, Derek decided that he wanted to become a pro baseball player. And he did not want to play for just any team. Derek wanted to play for the New York Yankees. In school, Derek told his classmates, "When I grow up, I'm going to be a shortstop for the New York Yankees."

After being drafted by the Yankees, the team invited the eighteen-year-old Jeter to Yankee Stadium. He compares gloves with Yankees Jim Leyritz (center) and Mike Gallego (right).

Derek's family supported his dream. His dad, Charles, often took young Derek to watch the Detroit Tigers play at nearby Tiger Stadium. Derek told his dad that he would someday be playing ball on the Tigers' home field. But he would be playing as a member of the Yankees rather than the Tigers!

While Derek's parents encouraged him, they made sure he stayed grounded. They told him he should not use the word "can't," because anything is possible. Derek's parents gave him a sense of self-confidence. Derek is biracial, as his father is black and his mother is white. Sometimes other kids made fun of the fact that he was different. But Derek's parents taught him to hold his head high. He learned that being different only made him more special.

The Jeters also made sure that Derek's schoolwork was more important than sports. If his grades were not good, Derek would have to give up baseball. Derek knew his parents were right. He worked hard in school. Derek was a top student and earned As on his report cards.

Jeter turns two against the Detroit Tigers. As a boy, Jeter's father used to take him to Detroit games at Tiger Stadium.

Basketball superstar Michael Jordan would later say about Derek, "I love his work ethic. He has a great attitude. He has the qualities that separate superstars from everyday people, and a lot of it is attributable to his great family background."

From left to right are Derek, his sister Sharlee, his mother Dorothy, and his father Dr. Charles Jeter.

By the time he reached junior high, Derek Jeter was a top athlete for his age group. He played both baseball and basketball. At age fourteen, Derek was playing varsity basketball. He had grown to six feet tall and was a great player. Once, Derek hit a three-point shot at the buzzer to win a basketball

Chapter 2

Growing Up

Derek Jeter blasts a home run off of Tampa Bay Rays pitcher David Price for his 3,000th career hit.

game for his team. But playing pro baseball was still his dream.

Derek was driven to achieve his goal. He practiced every day. In high school, he played shortstop, his favorite position. With his long arms, Derek was able to catch stray balls. And he could hit. In his junior year, Derek was batting .557! He also launched seven home runs that season.

Derek's strong arms came in handy, as he often had to clear snow from the baseball field in Kalamazoo. The snow and ice made the field slippery. As a senior, Derek was rounding first base one day when he slipped in an icy puddle and twisted his ankle. Derek was limping for weeks. But he refused to sit out. On a sore ankle, Derek batted .508 and averaged one RBI per game. He also stole 12 bases that season.

People around the country began to notice Derek's talent. That season, Derek was named High School Player of the Year. This award was given by the newspaper *USA Today*. He also won other awards. Derek was named the High School Player of the Year by the American Baseball Coaches Association. He

Jeter once played through an ankle injury during high school. But a more serious ankle injury would knock him out of the 2012 ALCS.

was given the High School Athlete of the Year award by Gatorade. Derek was even offered a full scholarship to the University of Michigan.

Derek knew that getting a college education was important. But it had been his lifelong dream to play big-league baseball. Pro scouts had been watching Derek's games. They wanted to see if Derek would fit well on their teams. The teams would pick players in the MLB draft. Most of the players in the draft were college players.

Derek was nervous on the day of the 1992 amateur draft. He was not sure if a team would take a chance on a high school player so early in the draft. The Houston Astros made the first pick. They chose Phil Nevin, a college star from Cal State Fullerton. Nevin would play 12 seasons in the major leagues, mostly with the San Diego Padres.

Four more teams made their picks, and each team chose a college player. Derek was not chosen. But Derek's favorite team, the New York Yankees, had the sixth pick in the draft. Finally, it was the Yankees' turn. And the New York Yankees selected Derek Jeter, the

Jeter was fortunate to have been drafted by his favorite team, the New York Yankees.

shortstop from Central High School in Kalamazoo, Michigan!

The Yankees phoned Derek at home with the news. He could hardly believe it. His lifelong dream was coming true. Derek was on his way to becoming a New York Yankee.

erek began his career with New York's minor-league team, the Gulf Coast Yankees. The team was based in Tampa, Florida. It was a long way from Kalamazoo, and Derek missed his family. He called his parents by phone every day. But he missed spending time with them.

Chapter 3

Living the Dream

Jeter signs autographs before a 2011 game as a member of the Trenton Thunder as he rehabs his way back to the major leagues. His first year in the minors was not as pleasant.

Standing on the Yankees dugout steps, Jeter poses after receiving the award for being named *Baseball America*'s 1994 Minor League Player of the Year.

Jeter struggled with the Gulf Coast Yankees. In his first game, he struck out several times. Hitting the ball was no longer easy. For the entire season, his batting average was only .202. The Yankees moved Jeter to another minor-league team, the Greensboro Hornets. They thought he would start hitting if he had more times at bat. He improved, but still had trouble hitting.

Jeter remembered what his parents had taught him. He was not a quitter. In the off-season, he worked even harder. He practiced hitting and fielding. Soon this extra work began to pay off. In his next season with the Hornets, Jeter was a different player. He hit five home runs, stole 18 bases, and had 71 RBIs. The managers voted him Most Outstanding Major League Prospect. He also earned a spot on the league's all-star team. *Baseball America* magazine named Jeter the "Best Defensive Shortstop," "Most Exciting Player," and "Best Infield Arm" at his level of minor-league ball. Soon he began moving up through the various levels of the minor leagues.

In 1994, Derek worked even harder. He hit .344 that season. He launched five home runs, stole 50 bases, and batted 68 RBIs. For his efforts, Jeter was named the Minor League Player of the Year by *Baseball America, The Sporting News, USA Today,* and Topps/NAPBL. He had proven he was ready to move up to the big league.

On May 29, 1995, Jeter played in his first major-league game filling in for the injured Tony Fernández. A thirteen-year veteran and four-time all-star, Fernández was the Yankees starting shortstop. Jeter did not have any hits that day. However, the next day he scored two runs

Chapter 4

Captain Clutch

A young Derek Jeter stretches before his first game with the New York Yankees.

and got two hits. Jeter played in 15 games that season before being sent back to the minor leagues.

The following season, first-year Yankees manager Joe Torre thought Jeter was ready to be the team's starting shortstop. At first, owner George Steinbrenner did not think Jeter was ready. But Torre and other members of the Yankees convinced him to give Jeter a chance. Derek Jeter started at shortstop before a huge crowd on Opening Day 1996.

Jeter did not let the fans down. In that Opening Day game, he launched his first MLB home run! That season, Jeter batted .314. He hit 10 home runs, scored 104 runs, and recorded 78 RBIs. At season's end, he was named the American League Rookie of the Year. Jeter received all twenty-eight first-place votes from the sportswriters who voted. Being named Rookie of the Year is a huge honor for any first-year player.

The Yankees made it to the postseason that year. Coach Torre knew he could count on Jeter. He placed Jeter in the leadoff batting spot in the lineup. In Game 1 of the 1996 American League Championship Series, the Yankees had fallen behind the Baltimore Orioles.

A young Yankees fan snags the ball Jeter hit before the Orioles right fielder can catch it. It was ruled a game-tying home run.

The score was 4-3 in the eighth inning when Jeter came up to the plate. Once again, Jeter wowed the fans. He hit a fly ball to right field. The ball was caught by a young Yankees fan before Orioles right fielder Tony Tarasco could grab it. Because the ball was out of play, the umpires ruled it a home run. The score was tied, 4-4. The Yankees won the game when Bernie Williams hit a home run in the bottom of the eleventh inning. New York then went on to win the series in five games.

From there, the Yankees went on to win the World Series. While some players struggled, Jeter played like a superstar. He batted .361 in the postseason to help the Yankees win the World Series over the Atlanta Braves. It was the first championship for the Yankees since 1978. That World Series win ushered in a new era of Yankees dominance.

In 1998, Jeter was named to play in his first MLB All-Star Game. He excelled during the regular season, leading the Yankees to 114 wins. For the second time in just three years, the Yankees made it to the World Series. Derek batted .353, and the Yankees defeated

Pumping his fist in celebration, Jeter rounds the bases after a home run in the 1997 ALDS.

the San Diego Padres in four games. The following season, 1999, Jeter led the Yankees to another World Series win over Atlanta. The Yankees swept the Braves in four straight games. For the series, Jeter batted an amazing .353. Just four seasons into his major-league career, Derek Jeter already had three World Series rings on his fingers.

Jeter just kept getting better and better. In 2000 he became the first Yankees player to be named All-Star Game MVP. Then he led the Yankees to yet another World Series win— this time over the New York Mets. Jeter became the only player to be

CHAPTER 5

Better and Better

Derek Jeter (right) with fellow Yankee greats Mariano Rivera (left) and Jorge Posada (center) standing behind the five World Series trophies that they won together.

Jeter makes a putout during Game 5 of the 2012 ALDS.

named All-Star Game MVP and World Series MVP in the same season.

Since that time, Jeter has proven to be one of the greatest baseball players ever. He led the Yankees to another World Series championship in 2009. That season he won many honors, including being named *Sport Illustrated* "Sportsman of the Year."

Jeter is one of the world's most popular athletes. He often appears in ads for all kinds of products. These range from Nike sneakers to Ford cars to Skippy peanut butter. The Avon Company even made a special Derek Jeter cologne.

After playing 17 full seasons, Derek Jeter showed no signs of slowing down. That is, until he broke his ankle during the 2012 ALCS. Still, in 2012, Jeter had 216 hits, the most of any player in MLB. Each year he continues to set new baseball records. Don Zimmer, a former coach for the Yankees, said: "(Derek Jeter) might go down, when it's all over, as the all-time Yankee."

As a member of the Yankees, Derek likes to win games. But he also knows that winning is not everything. From the time he was a young boy, Derek decided that he wanted to help other people. His favorite player, Dave Winfield, had his own charity foundation. Derek decided that he wanted to do the

Chapter 6

Making a Difference

During an event for his Turn 2 Foundation, Jeter surprised everyone by showing up and presenting them with gifts.

same. "When I make it," he said, "that's what I'm going to do."

Derek's dad, Charles, supported Derek's decision. In 1996, Derek and Charles sat down for pizza one night and talked about setting up a foundation. The charity would be called "the Turn 2 Foundation." The name was chosen partly because it is a baseball term. "Turning two" or to "turn two" is a reference to a double play in baseball. The name also represents a place for youngsters to "turn to" in place of drugs and alcohol. In its first year, Turn 2 raised $305,000 to help kids in need. Since then, it has raised more than $8 million dollars.

Besides the Turn 2 Foundation, Jeter often lends a hand with other charities. He holds the annual Derek Jeter Golf Classic to raise money for charity. He has donated sneakers to Soles4Souls, which provides shoes to needy kids. Jeter also hosts baseball clinics for inner city kids. When Derek reached his 3,000[th] hit in 2011, he partnered with the Movado watch company to donate the proceeds from a special "Derek Jeter" watch to charity.

CONGRATULATIONS
DEREK JETER

After Jeter's 3,000th career hit, Gillette made a $50,000 donation to the Turn 2 Foundation.

Derek Jeter salutes the fans after becoming the Yankees' all-time hits leader.

For his efforts, Derek has received many off-field awards. In 2012 he was given the Lou Gehrig Memorial Award. Lou Gehrig was one of the most famous members of the Yankees. He, like Jeter, was known for his kindness to others both on and off the field. Derek was honored to receive this award. (Derek has also bested Gehrig's record for the most hits as a Yankee!)

Derek Jeter helps people in any way that he can. He often visits sick kids in the hospital. He likes to talk to them and cheer them up. He kneels besides kids who are in wheelchairs and tells them that everything will be okay. He often brings them toys. He signs autographs for the older kids. Derek is truly a sports star who cares.

"People look up to you if you play for the Yankees," he once said. "I think you should do something to help out. Some players don't look at it that way. Off the field is when people look up to you even more. That's when your job starts. Baseball is the easy part."

Career Statistics

Year	Team	G	AB	R	H	2B	3B	HR	RBI	SB	AVG
1995	Yankees	15	48	5	12	4	1	0	7	0	.250
1996	Yankees	157	582	104	183	25	6	10	78	14	.314
1997	Yankees	159	654	116	190	31	7	10	70	23	.291
1998	Yankees	149	626	127	203	25	8	19	84	30	.324
1999	Yankees	158	627	134	219	37	9	24	102	19	.349
2000	Yankees	148	593	119	201	31	4	15	73	22	.339
2001	Yankees	150	614	110	191	35	3	21	74	27	.311
2002	Yankees	157	644	124	191	26	0	18	75	32	.297
2003	Yankees	119	482	87	156	25	3	10	52	11	.324
2004	Yankees	154	643	111	188	44	1	23	78	23	.292
2005	Yankees	159	654	122	202	25	5	19	70	14	.309
2006	Yankees	154	623	118	214	39	3	14	97	34	.343
2007	Yankees	156	639	102	206	39	4	12	73	15	.322
2008	Yankees	150	596	88	179	25	3	11	69	11	.300
2009	Yankees	153	634	107	212	27	1	18	66	30	.334
2010	Yankees	157	663	111	179	30	3	10	67	18	.270
2011	Yankees	131	546	84	162	24	4	6	61	16	.297
2012	Yankees	159	683	99	216	32	0	15	58	9	.316
	TOTALS	2,585	10,551	1,868	3,304	524	65	255	1,254	348	.313

G = Games
AB = At Bats
R = Runs
H = Hits

2B = Double
3B = Triple
HR = Home Runs

RBI = Runs Brought in
SB = Stolen Base
AVG = Average

Where to Write

DEREK JETER
C/O THE NEW YORK YANKEES
Yankee Stadium
161st St and River Ave
Bronx, NY 10452

All-Star Game—A game in which the best players from each league square off. The starters are chosen by the fans and the managers pick the reserves.

batting average—A player's number of hits divided by that player's number of at bats.

charity—An organization through which people donate time and money in an effort to aid those who are less fortunate.

diamond—A nickname for a baseball field given because of its diamond shape.

draft—A system by which team's choose amateur players to add to their organizations. The MLB Draft lasts forty rounds.

double play—The act of making two outs on the same play.

home run—A score made when a single player makes it all the way around the bases on a single hit.

leadoff—The first player to bat in the batting order.

MVP—Most valuable player on a team, in a league, or in a postseason series.

RBIs—Runs batted in.

run—A score made when a player makes it past first, second, and third base and to home plate, touching the bases in that order.

scout—An agent who searches for talented young players.

self-confidence—Belief in yourself and your talents.

shortstop—A player who fields between second and third base.

Soles4Souls—A charity that distributes pairs of shoes to those who cannot afford them.

Turn 2 Foundation—A foundation started by Derek Jeter that aims to help children avoid drugs and alcohol and have a healthier lifestyle.

varsity—A sports team representing a school or college.

World Series—The championship in Major League Baseball. It is held at the end of the season

Books

Jeter, Derek. *The Life You Imagine: Life Lessons for Achieving Your Dreams.* New York: Broadway Books, 2001.

Rappoport, Ken. *Derek Jeter: Champion Baseball Star.* Berkeley Heights, N.J.: Enslow Publishers, Inc., 2013.

Sheen, Barbara. *Derek Jeter.* Detroit, Mich.: Lucent Books, 2009.

Internet Addresses

Turn 2 Foundation

http://derekjeter.mlb.com/players/jeter_derek/turn_2_foundation.jsp

Derek Jeter Official Web Site

http://mlb.mlb.com/players/jeter_derek/index.jsp

New York Yankees Official Web Site

http://newyork.yankees.mlb.com/index.jsp?c_id=nyy

Index

A
Atlanta Braves, 31–33
Avon Company, 37

B
Baltimore Orioles, 29–31
Bradley, Ed, 7

C
Chicago White Sox, 5

D
Derek Jeter Golf Classic, 40
Detroit Tigers, 11

F
Fernández, Tony, 27
Ford, 37

G
Gehrig, Lou, 43
Greensboro Hornets, 25
Gulf Coast Yankees, 22–25

H
Houston Astros, 19

J
Jeter, Charles, 8–11, 40
Jeter, Derek,
   awards, honors, 17–19, 25–26, 29, 31, 34–37, 43
  birth, 8
    captain, 5
charity work, foundation, 40–43
debut, 27
nicknames, 7
position, 5–7, 9, 17
Jeter, Dorothy, 8
Jeter, Sharlee, 9
Jordan, Michael, 13

K
Kalamazoo, Michigan, 8, 17, 22
Konerko, Paul, 5

L
Little League, 9
Lou Gehrig Memorial Award, 43

M
Major League Baseball (MLB), 5, 37
MLB All-Star Game, 31
MLB All-Star Game MVP, 34–37
MLB Draft, 19
Movado watch company, 40

N
Nevin, Phil, 19
New York Mets, 5, 34
New York Yankees, 5, 9–11, 19–21, 22–25, 27–33, 34–37, 38, 43

Nike, 37

R
Rookie of the Year, 29

S
San Diego Padres, 33
60 Minutes, 7
Skippy peanut butter, 37
Soles4Souls, 40
Steinbrenner, George, 29

T
Tampa, Florida, 22
Tarasco, Tony, 31
Tiger Stadium, 11
Torre, Joe, 29
Turn 2 Foundation, 40

U
University of Michigan, 19
USA Today, 17

W
Williams, Bernie, 31
Winfield, Dave, 9, 38
World Series, 5–7, 31–33, 34, 37
World Series MVP, 37
Wright, David, 5

Y
Yankee Stadium, 9

Z
Zimmer, Don, 37

Derek Jeter
A Baseball Star Who Cares

Kimberly Gatto

Enslow Elementary
an imprint of
Enslow Publishers, Inc.
40 Industrial Road
Box 398
Berkeley Heights, NJ 07922
USA

http://www.enslow.com

Enlsow Elementary, an imprint of Enslow Publishers, Inc.

Enslow Elementary® is a registered trademark of Enslow Publishers, Inc.

Library of Congress Cataloging-in-Publication Data

Gatto, Kimberly.

Derek Jeter : a baseball star who cares / Kimberly Gatto.

pages cm. — (Sports stars who care)

Includes bibliographical references and index.

Summary: "Learn about Derek Jeter and how he knew when he was a child that he wanted to be where he is today. In this sports biography, follow Derek goes from becoming a great high school baseball player to an All-Star starting shortstop for the New York Yankees"—Provided by publisher.

ISBN 978-0-7660-4298-8 (alk. paper)

1. Jeter, Derek, 1974– —Juvenile literature. 2. Baseball players—United States—Biography—Juvenile literature. I. Title.

GV865.J48G48 2013

796.357092—dc23

[B]

2012047620

Future Editions
Paperback ISBN: 978-1-4644-0541-9
EPUB ISBN: 978-1-4645-1276-6
Single-User PDF ISBN: 978-1-4646-1276-3
Multi-User ISBN: 978-0-7660-5908-5

062013 Lake Book Manufacturing, Inc., Melrose Park, IL

Printed in the United States of America

10 9 8 7 6 5 4 3 2 1

To Our Readers:
We have done our best to make sure all Internet addresses in this book were active and appropriate when we went to press. However, the author and the Publisher have no control over, and assume no liability for, the material available on those Internet sites or on other Web sites they may link to. Any comments or suggestions can be sent by e-mail to comments@enslow.com or to the address on the back cover.

♻ Enslow Publishers, Inc., is committed to printing our books on recycled paper. The paper in every book contains 10% to 30% post-consumer waste (PCW). The cover board on the outside of each book contains 100% PCW. Our goal is to do our part to help young people and the environment too!

Photo Credits: AP Images/Bill Kostroun, p. 16; AP Images/Duane Burleson, p. 12; AP Images/Frank Franklin II, p. 42; AP Images/Gary Stewart, p. 28; AP Images/John Dunn, p. 32; AP Images/Julie Jacobson, pp. 1, 6; AP Images/*Kalamazoo Gazette*/Jonathon Gruenke, p. 39; AP Images/Mark Lennihan, pp. 24, 30; AP Images/Mel Evans, p. 23; AP Images/Paul Sancya, p. 18; AP Images/Richard Harbus, p. 10; AP Images/Rob Bennett/Gillette, p. 41; AP Images/Ron Frehm, p. 20; AP Images/Seth Wenig, p. 35; AP Images/Tomasso DeRosa, p. 36; Rena Schild/Shutterstock.com, p. 4.

Cover Photo: AP Images/Julie Jacobson